To Take and Have Not

A Sequence
of Idiomatic Poems

by
Keith Moul

ISBN-10: 098590285X
ISBN-13: 978-0-9859028-5-8

Written by Keith Moul
MoulPoemsPhotos@gmail.com

Book cover image by Keith Moul
MoulPoemsPhotos@gmail.com

Published by Broken Publications
www.BrokenPublications.com

For bulk order inquiries, please contact Broken Publications at:
www.BrokenPublications.com or
Jen@BrokenPublications.com

Broken Publications
PO Box 685
Eatonville, WA 98328

Other Titles by Keith Moul

Reconsidered Light (Broken Publications, 2012)

To Take and Have Not

Table of Contents

Acknowledgements

Many of these poems, in various earlier versions and more recently, have appeared in the following magazines:

Bacopa
Blue & Yellow Dog
Cirque Journal
Colorado State Review
*Ken*Again*
Menacing Hedge
Miller's Pond
Orion Headless
The Black Boot
The Cape Rock
Unfettered Verse
Write from Wrong Literary Magazine
Yakima

To Take and Have Not

His Flight

They agreed he was no thief,
although he often went alone
with opportunity; motive for others
had become impossible to ascribe:
but surely he had taken

flight

as always, a gift to his private cache:

a whistling feather,
a hollow bone,
the quest that loneliness allows;

white knuckles
in an adjacent seat,
palpable when taking off,
excruciating during landing;

ruthless dodges of gravity,
moral understanding,
perhaps love.

Recently he flew close to home,
in the neighborhood of her anxieties.
He let her choose as a pet
her preferred bird of apology.

Her Back Seat

They had agreed she was no thief,
but he caught a furtive gaze
that she could not surrender,
aging in her eyes,
when at last she took

a back seat

in the farthest reaches
of a vast arena
from where the warrior contest
offered only puppet show;
his voice was mere mouthing in the noise,
neither amplified nor echoing;
his fight pulsing out his blood.

So lonely in human fanaticism,
she stopped foolishly trying to hear.

Arisen in a new arena, she lived in
her hands, lively, graceful things;
her fingers long and flowing;
the clustered jewels
in her family ring.

His Bow

They agreed he was no thief,
but what about signs of vanity
that led to purpose without corruption?
When she arrived late again,
he seemed to be taking

a bow;

indeed,
deeply genuflecting;
scraping his stubby chin
to kiss her imagined, royal hem;
or backing off stage left
where wheezing critics waited,
rehearsed ambiguous praise.

The disputatious must disagree.
He will not snatch advantage:
crippling cowardice earns no Tony;
the vain man loathes a modesty – not
an eye in the house
is dry.

Her Chance Encounter

They agreed she was no thief,
although tempted by need, perhaps;
but much earlier, before their long intimacy,
they both urged new connections, on streets,
in cafes, on rock beaches of escape or pleasure;
he had heard her risk, then leapt to take

their chance encounter,

a minute taste first,
then gorging on him as her single sustenance.

She breakfasted and dined on love;
she lunched in private rooms
of joy; she never
missed a meal of him,
fixing each with special care.

Pulse far above normal,
she went to fat on faith in him,
succumbed to her heart beating
to a beat that floated, unattached,
and once attacked,
may refuse a second chance.

His Leaves

They agreed he was no thief:
he wandered the arboretum
looking up at fresh buds
exploding into bloom, nature's
spring into numberless distraction;

but surely he had taken

leaves

from those very sacred trees,
returned to arrange them lovingly
in wreathes about her bed.

They both slept with dreams,
each night an extraordinary ceremony.

The autumn alder contradicts its dream:
fall willows, maples shake toward dormancy;
the arboretum empties with their expectancy;
west winds enforce old laws in a new season.

Her Aim

They agreed she was no thief,
but with his quick feet and reliable zone,
he sensed her motion on the fly.

She had taken

aim,

pressured his best defense
with slashing cuts
and feather touch,
and scored
a canny shot;

or dead at his heart
to baffle his every sense,
all stunned
by her wizardry:

some games threatened injury,
some suffered abstraction,
even calculated war.

Her ardor was his anthem.

Himself Seriously

They agreed he was no thief,
not of the dangerous or petty type;
nor was he known for rank deceptions.
He would not troll for victims
at public events or without invitation,
even while lost for days on rural roads;
but surely he had taken

himself seriously

a major league prospect at 17,
eager to adore Houston, its Colts;
all set to bust baseball broncos
while legging doubles to the Hall of Fame;

in his Volkswagen van stage, bearded,
bristling at 22 with liberal arrogance
and herring-bone;

on a charming river,
isolated, even for Ontario,
loosed at 26 and armed
with a lever-action
Marlin .30-.30.
There he banged, then again.

She winced with him at 30,
during time's compulsive passing
when his foggy mirror
caricatured every altering feature
of his soggy morning face.

Her Liberties

They agreed she was no thief,
though often out of touch with time,
lost in hour-long minutes to abstraction,
but surely she had taken

liberties,

indulged every sense with exquisite bodies
that too assumed strange heights and compass
over her immediate space, visceral giants
engendered from her own horticulture.

His delight in temperaments of lilies,
her gardener's arrogance with aureoles,
to splash her blues, sow purples, lavish reds;
to throb in romantic war with adulteration.

She recalled an earlier valley,
faced toward temperate south
with earnest regard for compost.

Like the iris revealed in coils,
pendulous with an orange beard,
he stood by at full alert.

His Pages from Her Private Book

They agreed he was no thief.
He had no rap sheet, nor a single crime
in his long history laid against his name.
But surely he had taken

pages from her private book.

She was uncertain of where she left them,
how her usual tight security for privacy
had been violated. She felt violated.

He published them indiscriminately
for his fame, for his sympathy,
without acknowledgement.

She hoped her privacy was prize enough.

His invoked but inverted love as literary ravishment.
Like leaves that must dry and fall, she did not resist.

He touched her lips. They kissed.
Drowning after venturing too far
pulsed into her mind as an afterthought.

                    In print now,
they realized that lips may open
and be sublime, yet twist
into grotesque right after.

Her Cover

They agreed she was no thief,
but a barrage of doubts
had crippled her defenses,
especially so for a non-combatant.

She had taken

cover,

sheet, negligee, and pillow
to her survival room.

Thinking strange sounds
had come from her,
and to save the night,
she went to sleep alone.

He missed her.
He presumed the worst,
mostly of himself.

He left a post-it note
on the blank expanse of fridge
that he must go,
but he would hurry his return;
together again, each would find a haven.

His Heart

They agreed he was no thief;
nor a surgeon, nor anatomist,
nor master of complex *fauna*,
but surely he had sometimes taken

heart and other living organs

intimately in his gentle hands,
rotating them cautiously
as though in preparation
for dissection,
the surgical removal
of their failing parts.

These heart attacks occurred to her
when her garden lay drenched
under still-falling, redoubtable rain.

Then out of sorts, she wondered:
did her heart beat for his eye only,
in a richly elaborate China dish?

Her Time

They agreed she was no thief,
nor would she covet others' riches,
nor would she hoard adventure,
nor could she secrete celebrity,
but surely she had taken

her time

with a lioness possessiveness,
blood spattering her mouth and paws
for her evidence of ultimate tenacity.

Hunting season came earlier each year.
She appreciated birds at a respectful height
(unusual for a predator), flowers poking
through loam (absurd for a carnivore),
rain nurturing buds per natural urge
(potentially ruinous with obsessive behavior).

Yet in her flesh persisted a Serengeti heat,
a parch to dry the bones of naked prey:
animal inheritance witnessed on the plain,
essential to new seeds of presentiment
sprouting in deadly but consensual struggle.

In warming rain on her face and breasts
she fed in silence on her bountiful past;
let a beautiful present grow into her hands;
forecast a future forever dying and rebirthing.

His Time

They agreed he was no thief,
although he had slick tendencies;
he could escape latched relations;
he would circumvent others' logic;
he may in future offer ethics sales;
but surely he had taken

his time.

Little noticed by design,
he hid time in public places
that fired him secretly;
he fussed with time,
entirely as though his indoor cat;
he bounced time on a brick wall
as if his only child's rubber ball.
Then he boasted to her that,
undetected, uncontrolled, unrivaled,
his fire burned perpetually
without his adding fuel.

The willow goes dormant.
Paint peels on a solid house.
Insidious.

When time offers him no exit,
he braids long ropes of it;
his will to move circles, closets
in screaming rooms;
he cries that he is out of time.

Her Pains

They agreed she was no thief,
not with her respect for feeling;
but surely she had taken

pains.

Never to wear a badge of righteousness;
never with malicious spirit:

rather like a trash collector recovering
from a heap the rarest of all pains;
or one open to knowing accidental truth
who finds felicity behind his hurt;
or in a child's mood, unknowing
but hopeful of a mother's wisdom.
Yes, she secreted treasures in a cache—
never to display, ever mindful of duty,
ever respectful of how life will throb.

She allowed for candor and conscience.

His Taking Her Breath Away

They agreed he was no thief;
he completely lacked a gift
for larceny; he never could descend
from roof to window, nor arm
himself for potential confrontation.
But surely he had taken

her breath away:

air she shared in intimacy.

Any second her chest might cease
its rhythmic wave, her lungs implode
in the vacuum he bequeathed upon her.

She plied her breathless love
through city streets, in stuffy libraries,
down alleys of forgotten breezes;
she kept oxygen at hand
in cylinders like heavy ordnance;

she filled herself at will—
thought herself lighter by love,
easier with sighs, muscular for sex,
fueled for dives in darker reaches.

Her Turns for the Worse

They agreed she was no thief.
She did want more; she was not free
to appear as witness at national shrines,
to climb with her followers up mountains;
but surely she often swayed and had taken

turns for the worse

in labyrinthine tunnels of doubt;
then spun in reverse for the better,
or ran away through a winter forest.
Every turn attacked her equilibrium.

She loaded her suitcase with frozen memories.

She fought off rowdy neighborhood children
with a hoe, salesmen and burglars with a rake.

Her ailment seemed by now a favorite dog:
it had pit bull tendencies with dark red saliva.
Corridors of ominous doors refused entrance
to a woman brandishing a canine guard detail.

On wind, stray stories visited her,
stayed as houseguests for company,
like cats at ease with people, licked
kindness like icing from her fingers.

The neighbors kept a key near a window and
"kitty-kittied" to feed her actual cat.

His Refuge Again

They agreed he was no thief;
furtive, of course, choosing
as he sometimes did places
to wander among dark elements:
but surely he had taken

refuge

from her on a white day,
all brightness, all ambivalence—

so he holed up
in a billiard hall,
as a red ball clicked
off white balls,
all caroming
from cushion to cushion
by whiz following thud-thud-thud.

In this dark, still room,
among drowsy old men,
not caught but aligned to knowing,
he discovered everything:
three cushion mathematics,
perfect globes
on a soft field
of green felt:
a lighted universe
holding firm.

Her Refuge

They agreed she was no thief,
the kind always forced underground,
always stuck with the stick's short end
and making bad deals to avoid exposure:
but surely she had taken

refuge

as involuntary secretion from him
in the center of a crowded park
designed as classical minds favored,
with pale roses in ascendancy,
irises so showy in decline.

What she tended to there, roots tangled
with her private recollections of him,
roots now responsive to her fingertips,
talented with grit, subtly prospering
with manifestations new and admired.

The rockery gave witness to her strength.

Summer aromas filled old vacancies:
fullness left her peaceful.

Her Steps

They agreed she was no thief,
stepping in previous footprints
in flower beds outside the manor,
but surely she had taken

steps

much more plodding after and beyond change
than might seem necessary; to a knotted path
winding the sheer edge of derangement.

From cliff to tree, then to inner room where
her fingers stroked wood, metal, and vegetable
surfaces of things: the beige suede box
without a key; oriental poppies
rotting in a vase; the oak desk;
each of memorable grain
depicting its era,
set in her mind by physical sense,
not numbers in a column of dates.

Outside again, beyond the door,
the familiar street returns
to face her numbered house
as if from a wholly unnumbered,
unfamiliar place.

His Root

They agreed he was no thief,
but surely he had taken

root,

bole, branch, leaf, and abiding sap—
left one mummified log in the flame,
cedar snapping in her face
while fire glow innovates into ash.

At their hearth now,
she construes no more than a sum of parts;
she gazes at flickers, as a silent film;
she smells sweat on her paralyzed limbs;
she hears an intruder enter;
no second to escape, she feels
her molten eyes pour onto the stone.

Her Stock

They agreed she was no thief,
although she haunted storage rooms;
she preferred crime without violence on TV;
she collected hair conditioners for battered women;
but surely she had taken

stock,

although not fully apprised
at *that* minute
of the depth
of her investment.

Something was not right:
income was intermittent;
family and friends had hard times;
capital accrued became
paper unredeemable.

First she sold a family jewel
for less than its authorized appraisal;
then, her china, although heavy,
went substandard ways to other settings;
lately pawned a toaster, sans crumbs;
at last she tried
a flourishing rose
still connected to the earth.

New investment rules now seemed applicable:
equity in each transaction,
equality in all relations,
equilibrium dependent on functional lobes:
unreasonable frontal, spastic parietal,
blinded occipital, and delayed temporal;

she optioned on a dubious future.

His Taking it Upon Himself

They agreed he was no thief:
the IRS equated his return with honesty;
street kids sensed no concert in his choices;
veterans heard deferment, deduced disdain;
but surely he had taken

it upon himself,

as a man with life experiences will,
without consideration of gravity's burden,
without reference to timetables or maps,
without a thought of unintended consequences:

rapid bodily corruption of his athletic dash;
herniated discs up and down the lumbar:
callous fanatics driving nails
in and through his sciatic nerve.

Often before she had suggested
that, if his load should prove too much,
he should drop it where he stood.

Was he mortified to insist
that his pride was not a factor?

Her Taking Words Out of His Mouth

They agreed she was no thief,
but surely she had taken

the words out of his mouth,

as though words were gifts
at Christmas, fun for the unwrapping.

But this holiday especially portended
seasonal barrenness and a long silence;
led promptly to winter dormancy;
hard fatigues in the face of snow;
like the hunter, beyond hearing,
sighting but missing only a single rabbit.

Insulated securely in basements,
boxed and ready for another celebration,
even ornaments most prized
could break mysteriously.

His Taking Her by Surprise

They agreed he was no thief,
that between their moments together,
nothing would be missed nor added;
that when their torsos did not entwine,
there would be no winter of their souls;
that sirens were society's wail, not their screams;
but surely he had taken

her by surprise

when he burst into her presence, his
falsetto harmonizing with her fevered song;
when he spied on her enjoyment of herself,
later to confess his pleasure at her self-
awareness; when he wished
to accompany her for her own
epiphanies.

Her eyes craved surprises,
he learned after summer love;
her body contained its joy
for savoring later,
with him, and without shame.

Her Forever

They agreed she was no thief,
but in context of human life spans,
to which lounging gentlemen are subject,
surely she had taken

forever:

not ordinary relativity ("forever"),
but time from big bang through space
and curving relativity to black hole.

Uncomfortable with Einstein and dubious
of theoretical physics, he toyed with exaggeration!

If not early to rise or to the ball, when a second late,
in truth he might admit to complicity.

Both would promise earnestly,
but she could not fly and he could not wait;
two promises coordinate in consuming flames.

Minds at once merciful here are not well-met,
as if bereft and slaked in a desert,
too gritty for their surrounding sand;
seasons burst out and die in an instant;
convictions swirl in paradoxical air
as diaphanous as dust devils.

His Taking Turns for the Worse

They agreed he was no thief,
although a gamble might tempt,
although he jested butter-fingered larceny,
although inclined to better alternatives;
surely he had taken

turns for the worse.

His friends and neighbors lived perfect unease;
his siblings faced crises with corrections;
his town enjoyed all-American recognition.

So, his and her future could be somewhat flexible.

He cleverly compared their choices:
he as conductor on cross-country trains,
she as careerist tracking old delusions;
he as carpenter framing bathroom studs,
she as sea-nymph doing the backward crawl;
he as apologist projecting his silly humbugs,
she short on authority, softened his suffering.

Just there, mid-turn, worse pulled rank,
worked against his battling angels,
sabotaged his apologies with wanton pride.
In his case, she should not commiserate.

He often felt used badly by life, but
used to her little surprises, he tried
not to explain, not to seek accord.

Such bouts are short-lived,
whether evanescence or whirlwind,
but their toll in time debilitates.

His Taking Time

They agreed he was no thief,
at least not the broken-window,
slash-and-grab, bar-braggart kind
who sees triumph in a glass shard;
but surely he had taken

time,

likely to contain their accumulated gold;
time, a shared asset accruing interest;
time, coinage struck for obverse booms
with busts unremembered on reverses.

He squandered time on vainglory,
the most infuriating kind
that wears humility's mask.

Did he understand time's brevity,
its callousness toward its content,
its affair with the clock, ticking,
resounding in their time's empty cavity?

Did he acknowledge time's parody?

He turned comic of the twisted phrase,
capitalizing time's little beginnings
and punctuating time's grandiloquent pauses:
he was master of premature exclamations!

Could he resist time's seduction, the whore
letting him bargain for its favors
the way a young man will on a mean night,
the way time cheats, debases itself,
debases him?

When will time come around,
lawyer at hand, to be adjudicated?

Her Comfort

They agreed she was no thief—
friends refused release of her records
and he never thought to press.

But he became convinced that she had taken

comfort

in both sumptuous resorts of the mind
and squalid roadhouses of the heart,
according to democratic ideology.

She left messages promising
that solo vacations, although fun,
had victimized her in a wasteful phase
and that her work ethic would be revived.

And she fulfilled each promise
by always offering another promise
for the future; by learning
how to reinvent her past;
by helping him burlesque his past.

So what if she craved travel
to new but uncomfortable places?
She had the will to endure
and his will *should* go along:
                          both
supped the sweet joy of reminiscence.

Himself Too Seriously

They agreed he was no thief—
but surely he had taken

himself too seriously,

as if he alone guarded
prehistoric man's
single source of friendly fire.

He had said:
            "I am not so radical
            that I cannot excuse
            how little failures occur
            by our mutual consent;

                        I am not so serious
                        that I forget the wonder
                        of making amends and love –

                                    I have taken myself - seriously -
                                    to the edge of our community
                                    and walked home alone, in fog.

I am not so selfish
not to acknowledge
your contribution to my vision,
a lamp burning in the window
that welcomes me home."

Her Taking it as Her Right

They agreed she was no thief,
although some characters saw her
primed for villainous adventures,
flying well below the social radar.

Surely she must at times have taken

it as her right

to play the world, yet bet on wonder;
to seek or manufacture enduring bliss
and sit atop its throne like a queen.

Without architectural skill, he built
no monuments; he wore Halloween capes
and haunted the low places.

He never pretended to royal blood,
preferring to mock others' sucking
among walkups in the goblin alleys.

He mustered only childish hope
and wondered by what right
her sights aimed so high;

lower – many feet lower, in basements –
might her visions hit his heart dead center?

Her Hold

They agreed she was no thief,
but surely she had taken

hold

out of sovereign passion:
his whole world changed;
words he needed abandoned him;
images to excite registered in him
as drab, unnoticed, non-contextual.

Her worlds unzipped from his complacency;
she rode new erections of adopted primal force;
she exercised the lead in life's dance.

His vacuum of mind, spent by her desire,
limply accommodated her piercing inoculations.

Then she caged his body: on bread
and water alone, he climbed the walls;
he lost his motor control; he fixed
on abandoned mathematical theorems
as if ideas were indeed reality's resource;
he sought sanctuary, having forgotten
while under stress of love perverted,
God would restore his ascendancy.

Her Taking Him Straight

They agreed she was no thief,
prompt to assert her own beliefs,
achieving redress after her defeats;
but surely she had taken

him straight,

unadulterated, tempered by personal fire,
fanatic for the elemental: like gravity,
weak among natural forces, powerful
as water over falls,
tolerant of no obstacle,
relentless to the sea;

her own tears might torture her eyes,
her helpful fingers, her willing tongue;

he bent loyalty like a cheap spoon;
he tore regret from an ancient writ;
he twisted a great love.

Yet they fashioned obsidian
out of his occasional volcano.

His Polls

They agreed he was no thief,
ever contemptuous of felony,
transgression, or malefaction;
no ancient text controlled his life,
but he did devise his own meaning
of sin: in his politics, surely he had taken

polls.

Dutiful, he left home during winter,
foregoing warmth, foregoing affection,
foregoing needed repairs to his house:
only nails, not all voters, galvanized;
paint curdled, caulk was disposed
to desiccate, to expose architectural gaps.

Remote opinions mattered more
than mere delay of interior rot;
partisan oracles had seen harbingers in the breeze,
in flowing streams now clearing of cloudy silt.

She chafed.

Through pre-election haze, he trod
remote paths to remote houses cradled
by domestic smoke; occupants heartened
by truth, earnest although seldom witty,
that mistaken history would be rescinded;
that persuasive "leaders" be incapable of deceit;
that visitations would affirm their yeoman glory
in their rural rectitude. Goodness was at hand.

His need forced her strength, that her infirmities
may not impede his cause; that for truth she be there.
He would heed the winds proclaiming assent.

His Effect

They agreed he was no thief,
but the nature of their existence altered;
surely she met an unreliable world
at the second he had taken

effect:

the clock had tolled,
nothing stirred, complete silence;
the calendar had turned
to entirely new fateful events.

Had birds and butterflies
welcomed adaptation to ice?
Had violence as a lion
kneeled to the lamb?
Had children absconded
with light and innocence?

Or was it simply true
That, as our universe expands,
by necessity the backs come into view?

Intending self-destruction or not,
he devolved to fetal dependency;
he bled amniotic fluid;
he listed his possessions
and beliefs in his last testament
as "nil."

She finally accepted his panic
as more than, but inclusive of, private weakness;
as more than, but inclusive of
the reverse of a coin little known,
in spite of the demand for the obverse;
like more than, but inclusive of, a hurt evangelist,
disoriented, committing faithless acts
usual only to nonbelievers.

Her Lessons

They agreed she was no thief,
no gypsy nor homeless troubadour
pursuing sonorous accents and quips,
but surely she had taken

lessons

from those whom she trusted,
but as often she self-taught,
as though life were a guitar
for diversion, not the concert stage;
tuned, stringed tight, and fretted;
requiring callouses for comfort,
nimble fingers pursuing basic chords
and caution with sharps and flats.

He could not know without asking
if her longing to perform went deep
as breath in farther reaches of her lungs,
or shallow as sounds of hyperventilation.

As her nonverbal answer,
she relegated her guitar to gather dust;
but she kept it handy, if resonant sound
might be revived to tip domestic scales.

His Lessons

They agreed he was no thief,
no pickpocket nor heroic Lancelot,
but surely he had taken

lessons

from people professing truth,
as if revelations occurred
at planned intervals,
such as the 11:27 arrival
at Coupeville
of the Port Townsend Ferry.

Fortunately, a simple reservation
might help him deal with insatiable learners
clogging the lowered ramp
and the public waiting area,
buzzing with walk-on traffic
for Whidbey Island.

But the Tuesday sailing
included no eager crowd,
some with, some without reservations;
it left in light fog, still surfaces,
even somberly: what truth
could be in this? A mechanical conveyance,
its small crew on yet another passage,
passengers with their needed coffee
at the second deck cafeteria,
speaking at engine rhythms and steady
lopping of the bow through choppy waves;
the sacrifice of truth to life's continuum,
learning's titillations, to damp redundancies
of orderly embarking, orderly disembarking,

strict compliance with time's exigencies,
no first, nor second, coming on a wave.

His Umbrage

They agreed he was no thief,
in a context frankly feudal,

but surely he had taken

umbrage

at her most independent moment,
when idea conflates with action,
organic in its genius.

He squalled impetuous squalls,
tried to split the course of her river
into small streams, each
collecting at his dams.

Finally, there he built his castle,
stocked his keep, hid away
a votive altar, at which
he chose few among many
petitioners to worship.

Uncalled, her mind flayed,
she cancelled her pilgrimage,
reasoning that stone
mortared to stone
may be important work,
but certainly no miracle.

His Taking Up Residence

They agreed he was no thief,
although perhaps unwise in living
arrangements, permanent or temporary;
but surely he had taken

up residence

in a Saxon farmhouse during a moment
of splintering – even collapsing – mind,
on a hill fostering medieval illusions,
overlooking peasant fields of meagerness.

Like a boisterous crow visiting a baleful place,
he swaggered to and hopped over carrion,
filled himself with no concern for rottenness;
then he flew to the one surviving tree to observe.

She watched, too, but while caught in a skirmish
of ordinary folk who were "not so queer;"
she dodged their rocks and clubs until the dark.

Chuckling, he chronicled the action.

With paper so dear, writing rare, she chose
to offer no contradicting version of events.

Her Defensive Position

They agreed she was no thief,
although she was sly, often adept
at psychological slight of hand,
particularly cunning with wordplay,
but surely she had taken

a defensive position

beyond metaphorical hypotheses,
with metaphysical ramparts
(that had always been *his* passion),
a working drawbridge, and mawkish moat.

He was, of course, at a loss in such circumstances.
She was never to him "the little lady," but
from whence had this Amazon emerged, mailed,
with battle axe and shield? Even a loyal page?

He had to sit and thrum his lute.

Would she relent and feast? She would.

His Comfort

They agreed he was no thief,
but when ambient light was weak
and could not expose his sunken eyes,

suspicion seized her
that he rushed to take

comfort

in pliable attitudes
that he called "free expression,"
since ratification his constitutional right;
she called them "license"
and, after all, how to help reconcile
those views in the child's pliable mind?

He often thought of the child,
she demanding, he demanding her
immersion into diversity, suggesting
that she read the signs; begging
her compassion for oddity
of all kinds, then bent down
begging her forgiveness.

Years passed.

He pleaded that they both consider
how they knew and what
was still hidden from them; when
to accept or reject perceptions;
whether to go along with
or resist temptations;
how his anguish had become theirs.

True, life became strange,
uncomfortably hard as diamond.

Her Stand

They agreed she was no thief.
She may even possess a thief's genes,
but her upbringing, her parents, her siblings,
her daughter, and her husband abhorred
felonies while not too aware of misdemeanors.

But surely she had taken

a stand,

not at a one-way window viewing suspects,
or looking back at the window, accuser concealed,
but on life principles she had intuited, wrested
from events in her experience, stolen perhaps
from others' experiences, even found in gutters.

Everyone must age, everyone must die. No one
can forever avoid the stages of grief. *Handcuff me,*
she thought, *drag me before the judge. I'll take
the stand, I'll enter my plea, I'll defend myself.*

His Refuge

They agreed he was no thief,
but surely he had taken

refuge

in a private place,
to which he denied her access.
He had secreted himself in his bunker.
He had issued mad orders.
He had studied legal precedent
and drafted singular laws
that lawyers would praise.
He had refused to accept, sometimes
even small tokens of her love.

For reasons clear only to her,
facing his abuse, denials and refusals,
facing hours empty of her preferred him,
she still made his excuses,
she still thought dutifully of the future.

He failed to make her his victim.
She contracted pieces of madness,
but with honor and a shield of dignity,
admired by family and remaining friends.

Her Fall

They agreed she was no thief
as she wobbled on Grand Canyon's north face,
even at windows above two floors in small cities,
making her not a candidate for burglary;
but surely she had taken

a fall

at some moments before the world's judgment,
a misstep along duty's line as she saw it,
or extended past her grip on her mental tether;
she just felt rightly that it was her time to fly.

Not all such falls are survivable.
He counseled her that if she could survive
(and he couldn't ask for a better outcome),
He, too, had needed to jump into airs of crisis,
like her tempting plots, even reprisals.

There would of necessity be breaking and scarring;
nightmares and more ordinary conditioned recall,
but she felt more at ease with failure, and success.

His Steps

They agreed he was no thief.
He may walk quietly, never skulk.
When still young he could be shy.
But surely he had taken

steps

further than scientifically sound
from measurable, magnetic center
to the far edge of lovers' orbits;
then bore at her at high speed,
steel arrow heated at steep re-entry,
very close but inches short of heart;

and then, perhaps in giddy embarrassment,
he choreographed for her a curious dance
that he called a *soft-shoe waltz,*
clumsy with pirouettes, given his physique;

all for pure release and farcical remorse;
his sinews hurt, burning in personal flame.

Her Hint

They agreed she was no thief,
but when a girl, adolescent things appealed;
when still a young adult, mature ideas
rushed in like sexual tides surrounding islands
of adolescent things; from these she took

a hint:

some futures must be forbidden, whether by
relevant texts, sage advice, or common sense.

Yet, as church bells rang, she tingled; sun on maple leaves
stippled through shadow to pungent ground;
cataracts on a local stream teased her ins and outs;
she heard melodies near her breasts and loins;
she felt immobile before inchoate moving figures.

At the ebb, she had reached many disparate conclusions,
paradoxes, blind alley contradictions, lifetime frustrations.

She never knew cunning, but by then made due with hints.

His Vow

They agreed he was no thief,
but so often things went missing,
subtly important or symbolic things
to one or the other of them, or both,
presentiments of different things to come.

His natural diffidence
made his promises common,
fulfillment of his promises rare.
How ordinary reliance on tact
had in this failed him so, who knows.

For repose, he closed
his eyes and took

a vow

to vast and unknowable space,
regarding lost things, mislaid ideals,
misdemeanors likely unremedied.

She questioned, "Why?" challenge long intimacy,
"Why?" expose long unspoken efficacies?
"What?" defenses could evade
charges of more serious felonies?

Their privacy now antecedent to public abuse,
"When?" would their lives speed past light
as forecast of the expanding universe?
"Who?" would they by then have become?
And, "Where?" in which gods' minds
could parallels in being finally be achieved?

Would old, petty crimes be forgiven?
Could they rely on chance to re-purpose expectations?

Yes, he had vowed to limitless space;
yes, he welcomed her to occupy it with him.

He confessed to her that *he* thought of life
as a gift of terrible beauty and beyond which
he conceived no more to offer her.

Her Vow

They agreed she was no thief
and past had always been prelude
to their present; but she had soared
as if waxen near heat; and now she took

a vow

that, despite her risk, her heights
aided her dizzy energy in flight;
new boundaries, or none at all,
re-defined her sphere of interest;
a pure summons to thrones of gods
made her consort to infallibility.

He, on course to his own universe of disappointments,
smarted from her personal lessons, bore
molecules to ions of her charged atmosphere;
consented to her journey, though it mean
a limited partnership in life's transactions.

If the fall were to the sea,
all would clamber to avoid a *tsunami*.

About the Author

Keith Moul will be 69 years old in November, 2014. After working in the insurance business as a company manager, he has retired and finally settled in a very comfortable niche. He writes poems and takes photos with Port Angeles, WA as his base, travelling quite frequently with Sylvia, his wife, or alone, just to enjoy looking at things. *To Take and Have Not* is his fourth volume of poetry since 2010. A fifth book, *Theodore Roethke's Career: an Annotated Bibliography*, is almost ancient history now, having been published in 1977.

www.ingramcontent.com/pod-product-compliance
Lightning Source LLC
Chambersburg PA
CBHW071641040426
42452CB00009B/1722

* 9 7 8 0 9 8 5 9 0 2 8 5 8 *